Between
TIME
and
Meaning

A. René Whitaker

Between TIME and Meaning

Copyright © 2016 by A. René Whitaker

Published by Whitaker Press

Cover design by Josh Simonis
All rights reserved.

ISBN-13: 978-0-9976216-0-0
ISBN-10: 0-9976216-0-5

Dedication

This book is dedicated to
Margaret Cook
who encouraged me to
write, write, write.
In addition, it is dedicated to
my mother, who has
supported me during all
the hills and valleys of my life.

TABLE OF CONTENTS

Introduction

The poems on the following pages continue
the story of a personal journey of hope
and healing, which was witnessed to in my
first book entitled, Gravity, Gratitude, Grace.

These poems reflect a time in-between.
The trauma has passed, but the future has
yet to unfold. It is a time of waiting and
reflection. In the pages that follow you
will find gifts from the One source of all
life and love. I hope that they will
provide a cradle of comfort as you travel
in your own time in-between.

Time In-Between

The time in-between is a
puzzle of promise
and possibility
No longer stuck by sadness
Happiness is a ways away
Time is precious
All is pressing toward
a new purpose
But it isn't yet revealed.

DAY ONE

Moments of Meaning

Moments of meaning
Make up a life
Often small measures
Of kindness
Thoughtful preparations
Chance encounters
Risks with rewards unknown
What more is life really?
But small moments
Of meaning
Woven together
Over the course of the years.

DAY TWO

A Little Mercy

It is mercy that we need
A little compassion please
Not anger or judgment
But love you see
A little mercy would be nice
Along with kindness too
Can I share it with myself
Or offer it to you?
Can I find an ounce of mercy
Just for me today?
Or is that too much to ask?
It wasn't how we were raised.
Who would know its such
An arduous task
To offer mercy inside and out.
We proclaim it's what our faith
Is all about.
But do we offer mercy?
Do we even know how?
Follow Jesus on the path
Where it is shown
Here, there and now.

DAY THREE

Beyond the Tornado

Like a tornado
A wind blew through my world
And tore it apart
Pieces scattered here and there
A hole left in my heart

Rebuilding is not so simple
But something we must do
With a board, a brick
And emotional glue

The pieces return to where
They've never been
Newness of life
Lets you start once again

Build stronger and tighter
Than ever before
On a solid foundation
Which God has restored.

DAY FOUR

Fear and Courage

I keep being afraid
I'm doing it wrong
My life I mean
But wrong according to what scale
Who decides if a life is right
Or less than what we expect?
I don't know but it is someone
In my head who is embarrassed
That I haven't lived another way
Yet, I don't know how to live except
How God made me to be.
So is it courage to be who we are
Meant to be when others say,
"Not that way."
I don't know.
Sometimes it feels like crap.
That's all I can say.

DAY FIVE

Gray, Fuzzy Fog
Gray, Fuzzy Fog of Fear
Surrounds my thinking
About these words
Have   Have Not
Is having okay?
Having what?
What do I have?
I seem to have a lot of fear
That masks what else I have
Courage
Strength
Resilience
Determination
Intelligence
Creativity
Imagination
Faith
Hope
Love
Why do I seem to stop with the fear?
Where do you stop?
What do you have within you today?

5

DAY SIX

Collateral Damage

How does one rebuild
When the home is broken
By others and
You are just collateral damage?
Do you count?
Do I count?
Does it matter?
Is that what they wondered too?
Do we count?
Does it matter?
Is that what they were asking
But their pain got in the way
And they took it out on someone else?
But what we want to know is:
Do I count?
Do I matter to me?
Did I matter to you?

DAY SEVEN

Falling from Calling

I fell from my call or
Was I pushed, prodded and pulled?
Left to bear the pain alone.
No wonder I feel so abused.
Yet, I wasn't alone with prayers
From far and near.
And God calls through the pain
So we can see more clearly
The possibilities that await
Just outside the inner door
Making ready our leap
Back into our call again.

DAY EIGHT

China Dolls

Like china dolls dropped and shattered
Glued together but not quite right
Compassion for others
Less so for self
Lifted up for healing
From where will it come?
Fragile, fragile, but strong as well.
Compassion for self
Is slow to emerge.
But healing comes with
Teardrops and love
And time and prayer.

DAY NINE

Holy Broken

If I am broken
Can I be made whole?
Or am I whole in my
Brokenness?
What does this have to do
With anything?
Or does it have to do with
Everything?
What don't I understand?
Or is there anything to
Understand?
Is it simply how life is?
Who can help?
Where to turn?
What are the things you
Can do when you
Are afraid?
What about what God
Can do?
Will God send someone
To help repair the brokenness
Or
At least love us no matter what?

DAY TEN

Revelation

The revelation allows us to
Recreate
Rehabilitate
Renew

Reorganize
Reenergize
Restore

Renovate
Rejuvenate
Rejoice

Reinvigorate
Reevaluate
Refresh

So that resurrection
Can make us new.

DAY ELEVEN

Parts and Whole

Leaf, Tree, Petal, Flower
The parts. The whole.
They are separate.
They are one.
Like people and not.
Is it a tree without any leaves?
Or a flower without petals?
Are we someone without others?
Leaf, Tree, Petal, Flower

DAY TWELVE

Home
Home has been many places
And no place at all
Where have I felt at home?
Grandma's house
Church
St. Charles
With husband
With friends
School
Seeking
Safety
Not
Suffocation
Longing for place
Not knowing anywhere
But hoping for heaven
In whatever form that will be
In this moment I am at home
With my mom and Trinity.
We are okay.

.

DAY THIRTEEN

I Am Like
I am like
A creative ornament
A sad clown
A hurting human
A preaching fool
A fragile female
A sacred vessel of love
A needy child
A loving friend
A curious category

I am like all of these
And more
What are you like?
Are we the same or different
Perhaps it is both
and
or

DAY FOURTEEN

Identity Pieces

Identity pieces scattered about
Makes me want to scream and shout
How did it happen?
What did I do?
To bring on the pain as if covered with glue.
Did I trust too much
Or just the wrong sort
Was I going too fast
Or stop too short?
All I know is it hurts like hell.
Wondering now if I'll ever feel swell.

Were my thoughts not right?
My emotions too tight?
Was there really something wrong with me?
Can I change it anyway? Can you see?
Who do I trust? Which way to turn?
Is there something new that I must learn?
Change what you can.
Leave the rest well alone.
How can we know what's left to be done?

Care and prayer and living today.
It seems so trite, but it's all I can say.
No grand solutions. No simple phrase.
One can't go forward on endless clichés.
Since we can't go back go forward we must.
All we need is some courage and a smidgen of trust.

DAY FIFTEEN

Leaver and Left

The leaver and the left behind are hurt
along the way
One may plan and make escape
The other just shocked that day
The pain is real for both you see
Although it comes in different shapes.
If all was well, would you just go
And leave behind the drapes
plus all your hopes and dreams and such
To start it all again?
Yet you won't know what it is you've lost
Until it's done and gone.
Once the choice is made what was
has all but come undone
The leaver and the left behind
are hurt in different ways
The pain is there until it's not
for an untold number of days.

DAY SIXTEEN

forgive
forgive
what you know
and
what you don't know
so you can let
it go and live,
live, live
not easy
it is true
but do it for you
if you forgive
you can live anew.

DAY SEVENTEEN

Favorite Words

Can you name a favorite word
Or even two or ten?
Where will you start a list
Perhaps almost at the end
Where the zenith lives
Or is it a zoo?
Can you hear me now?
I'm talking to you.
Do you have a word you love
Or one that makes you smile?
How often will you use it
Everyday or just once in a while?
Does it trip off your tongue
Or twist all around?
When you use it how
Wonderful might it sound?
Or is it a word with meaning
And the sound is not so great.
I'd really like to know
So tell me, don't even hesitate.

DAY EIGHTEEN

Loss and Laughter

Where is the grace to grieve
The loss that makes no sense?
We want to say we understand
To put it in its place
When love just disappears
What's left but empty space?

My mind just won't let it be.
It seeks a meaning now.
But no matter what I think
I don't quite get the why or how.

How could a person just say, adieu,
Without a reason why?
I'll never understand it.
Perhaps I shouldn't try.

I don't just grieve the loss of one
Who made me laugh and smile.
My tears are shed for who I was.
I haven't seen her in awhile.

I used to have a carefree heart
But now my heart's afraid to care.
So offer me grace today
And let me shed some tears.

Tomorrow the happiness will be reborn
And light my path again.
I feel a smile rise up inside
So let the laughter begin!

DAY NINETEEN

Matrix Theory
I don't understand
What all was lost
I want to understand
But this loss is as complex
As matrix theory.
I know the words
But when they are put together
They don't make any sense.
No sense that feels like nonsense
And I cannot quite give myself
The grace I need to grieve
And so it comes in fits and spurts.
Along with healing and hope
And perhaps even happiness …

DAY TWENTY

Dangerous to Disagree
It is dangerous to disagree
Especially when you are fragile
For someone will pounce on it
And take away any measure of comfort
Safety seems to lie in always being
the same
as others
But what if you are not?

What if you are tall and
They are short
Or the other way around?
What if your hair is dark
and hers is light?
How do you stand your ground?
What if your demeanor
is serious and silly
But in a different way?
What if you are smart
and they aren't quite so?
How do you fit in
as the same except
to play dumb or
Keep quiet?

So we seek new places
where we might belong
And believe
it isn't so dangerous
to be who we are
Or were all along.

DAY TWENTY-ONE

Small Things
Where is safety?
In small things
Like clean sheets
And walking the dog
Eating lunch with a friend
Reading a good book
Writing whatever is
Feeling wanted
Being needed
It is these every day activities
And connections
That keep us safe.

DAY TWENTY-TWO

The Bottom
I see the bottom
I am no longer there
But I am afraid
I may fall again
I'm not sure how
To let go of or heal
That feeling.
So I write it out.
It is the fear of falling
That keeps me stuck
Somewhere
Down here
So I have to find the
Courage to climb
Without looking
Down or back
Just keep climbing
Even when you are afraid
The fear will seem to disappear.

DAY TWENTY-THREE

Stuck in the Flow

I get stuck in the feelings
Because it seems to take
Too long to let them flow
But in remaking a life
How else can we ever know
If we don't share those feelings
Or the thoughts that they bring
Together they make a life
Where we laugh, cry and sing.

DAY TWENTY-FOUR

Center on Hope

A beautiful newness has begun
It is filled with scary freedom
To begin again and again once more
Something forgotten and
now remembered
In this time of renewal
Center on hope
Trusting in the One
Who has come
And who lives and breathes
In me and you and us
Watch the unfolding
As it blossoms and blooms
Saying:
Wow!
Thank you!
Amen.

DAY TWENTY-FIVE

Spelling Errors

Don't you just love spelling errors?
They can may you laugh or thunk
Or was it think?
Maybe you'll at rather than eat
Or rink instead of drink.
Sometimes you find
The Jesus instead of then.
But it isn't a random Jesus
So why even pretend
Thant spelling errors aren't
A part of everyday life
When we discover them.
Let's share a simple smile
And let go of any strife.
Hee hee!

DAY TWENTY-SIX

Roller Skates

Freedom dashed
Trapped and clinging
Feet slipping
What if no one comes?
Trapped because the skates
On my feet slipped
under the car
I was not alone
even if I was afraid.
And then her big brother
Came to help me out.
But skating was never the same.

DAY TWENTY-SEVEN

Toys

When is the last time
I had a toy I loved?
That helped me play
And laugh and sing?
Where are the toys?
Where is the fun?
Can I laugh with ease again?
And remember how to
Enjoy life and even love?

When is the last time
You had a toy you loved?
That helped you play
And laugh and sing?
Where are the toys?
Where is the fun?
Can you laugh again today
And remember how to
Enjoy life and even love?

DAY TWENTY-EIGHT

Connections
Connections, connections
Come from many directions.
How do we learn to belong?
Reaching out however we can
Whether we're weak or so strong.
We need to connect whoever,
wherever we are.
Sometimes we are near
Other times they are far.
Pictures of an odometer
from a land far away
Tell us more than words alone
can barely begin to say
What draws us together
Rather than tears us apart
Can we begin by expanding
our hearts?
Then we may see how
breath, word or string
weaves us together
Reminding us
we are connected
through the Source
of all things.

DAY TWENTY-NINE

The Wall

Whether it is a wall or a well
One must climb to get over or out
They both keep us from seeing
What's ahead.
So we must climb without knowing
What waits for us.
We climb with our courage and our fear.
We climb because we can't stay here
Stuck and too afraid to move.

To Climb

To climb means to move
It takes strength and courage
I haven't done much
Physical climbing
Because I was afraid
Afraid of falling once I climb
Afraid that I'm not good
Enough or strong enough
So I get stuck along the way
But today I climb. Do you?

DAY THIRTY

The Essentials
Bed, Desk, Dog, Car
Down to the essence of my life
Sleep and rest
Talk with a friend or two
Write each day
Talk with a friend or two
Take the dog for walks
Walk me too
For health and solace
Sometimes we go for a ride in the car
Bed, Desk, Dog, Car

.

DAY THIRTY-ONE

The Gift

Remember the gift.
It is called life.
Too often taken for granted.
When we say, "thank you"
We offer our gratitude.
Is it enough?
What else do we have to give?
I want to be enough
In return for this gift called life.
And if I am not,
May God forgive me
And still offer me grace again today

A BRAND NEW DAY!
Road Travelled Less

Who plans on taking that road
travelled less? Not I.
Who wakes one day and looks ahead
To see it differently. Not me.
Choices are set before us.
Advice and wisdom shared.
We take one step and then two more
That unworn path is dared.
We could turn back. But why not go on
And see what's up ahead?
We will never know what might have been
Had we gone where the smooth path led.
So we open our eyes and look around.
That unknown world does shine
But causes a glare so we can't quite see
The way we think we should
Yet the journey for us will be truly sublime
If we don't compare
Or expect what's not there
But accept what comes each day.
No one said it would be easy
Only that we would learn much
As we travel along the way.
Let's take a few sure steps
And then some more tomorrow
Together with our trusted friends
We'll find a life lived with both
Joy and sorrow
That path may be travelled less
We know it may be true
It doesn't mean its any worse or better
Just that it's right for you.

About the Author

Rev. Dr. A. René Whitaker is an ordained Presbyterian minister. She has worked with congregations in transition for 15 years. Rev. Whitaker earned a Master of Divinity at Austin Presbyterian Theological Seminary. In 2014, she completed a Doctor of Ministry in Science and Theology at Pittsburgh Theological Seminary. Her final project is entitled, Creating Community in a Networked World.

Rev. Whitaker is currently serving a congregation in Michigan. She is also available to lead retreats, preach and offer spiritual care. Her first book, *Gravity, Gratitude, Grace: A Journey of Healing & Hope* was published in 2012. Other publications are on the way.

A Poem of Your Own

www.ingramcontent.com/pod-product-compliance
Lightning Source LLC
Chambersburg PA
CBHW071751020426
42331CB00008B/2277